Bloom's Taxonomy & Depth of Knowledge Charts

Compiled by: Tracy Jarboe & Stefani Sadler

Illustrated by: Stefani Sadler

ABCschoolhouse

Copyright © 2012 by abcschoolhouse.com

Many teachers are now asked to turn in, or post, lesson plans as part of their professional expectations. For many, it is an expectation to also include Bloom's or Depth-of-Knowledge Levels alongside learning targets/objectives. To support teachers with this expectation, we have designed posters/charts to meet this need. This e-book contains a set of color and a set of black/white charts for both the traditional and revised Bloom's Taxonomy and Depth of Knowledge. These charts may be used in their current 8.5" x 11" form or enlarged to create classroom posters. We have also provided graphic cards for your own creative classroom use. This e-book is 47 pages in length.

Tips

- Save this e-book to a file on your computer as soon as possible. Your download privileges are time sensitive.

- Only print the pages you need as you need them. Printing the entire book will use a great deal of paper and ink.

- Make a master file of the pages you print to use again next year.

- If a page becomes lost, don't worry as you will have the master file saved on your computer.

Dear Teachers,

We have worked diligently creating this packet for you. We hope you are excited about these activities and enjoy using them in your classroom. We kindly ask that you honor the copyright of our materials and do not "freely share" this packet with your friends and colleagues. If others like these activities as well, simply refer them to the website at which you purchased yours and they may purchase a set as well. When copyrighted materials are photocopied for, or emailed to others, this is not only breaking the law, it is just not nice. We want to continue providing materials for you at an affordable cost. Thank you for your thoughtful consideration of copyright.

Copyright © 2012 by Stefani Sadler and Tracy Jarboe

All rights reserved. **No** part of this book other than the specified blackline masters may be reproduced mechanically, electronically, photocopying or any other means without prior written consent, except in the case of book reviews. The specified blackline masters may only be reproduced for the purchaser's individual classroom use and may not be used for school-wide or district distribution without prior written permission from ABC Schoolhouse. Additional copies of this publication are available online through the abcschoolhouse.com, teacherspayteachers.com, or atozteacherstuff.com websites.

Bloom's Taxonomy: A quick overview

"Bloom's Taxonomy" is a classification of the educational learning objectives that teachers set for students. It was proposed in 1956 by a committee of educators chaired by Benjamin Bloom and has since been revised. Bloom's divides education objectives into 3 domains the cognitive (knowing/head), the affective (feeling/heart), and the psychomotor (doing/hands). There are 6 levels in Bloom's taxonomy, moving from the lowest order processes to the highest.

1. **Knowledge**: Basic knowledge demonstrated by memory or recall of previously learned material: recalling facts, terms, basic concepts, and answers. (count, define, describe, draw, find, identify, label, list, match, name, quote, recall, recite, sequence, tell, and write)

2. **Comprehension**: Demonstrative understanding of facts and ideas by organizing, comparing, translating, interpreting, giving descriptions, and stating main ideas. (conclude, demonstrate, discuss, explain, generalize, identify, illustrate, interpret, paraphrase, predict, report, restate, estimate, rewrite, review, summarize, and tell)

3. **Application**: Using new knowledge to solve problems to new situations by applying acquired knowledge, facts, techniques, and rules in a different way. (apply, change, choose, compute, construct, dramatize, interview, prepare, produce, role-play, select, show, transfer, and use)

4. **Analysis**: Examine and break information into parts by identifying motives or causes, or make inferences and find evidence to support generalizations and answer why. (analyze, break down, characterize, classify, compare, contrast, debate, deduce, diagram, differentiate, discriminate, distinguish, examine, outline, relate, research, and separate)

5. **Synthesis**: Compile information together in a different way by combining elements in a new pattern or proposing alternative solutions. (compose, construct, create, design, develop, integrate, invent, make, organize, perform, plan, produce, propose, and rewrite)

6. **Evaluation**: Present and defend opinions and make judgments about information, validity of ideas, or quality of work based on a set of criteria. (appraise, argue, assess, choose, conclude, critique, decide, evaluate, judge, justify, predict, prioritize, prove, rank, rate, and select)

* **Bloom's Taxonomy** was later revised to the following format: 1. **Remembering** (Knowledge) 2. **Understanding** (Comprehension) 3. **Applying** (Application) 4. **Analyzing** (Analysis) 5. **Evaluating** (Evaluation) 6. **Creating** (Synthesis)

Depth of Knowledge: A quick overview

According to Norman L. Webb interpreting and assigning Depth-of-Knowledge levels to both objectives within standards and assessment items is an essential requirement of alignment analysis. There are 4 levels of Depth-of-Knowledge.

READING

Level 1 requires students to use simple skills or abilities to recall or locate facts from the text. The focus is on basic initial comprehension, not on analysis or interpretation. Items require only a shallow or literal understanding of text presented and often consist of verbatim recall from text, or simple understanding of a single word or phrase.

Level 2 requires both initial comprehension and subsequent processing of text or portions of text. Important concepts are covered, but not in a complex way. Items at this level may include words such as: paraphrase, summarize, interpret, infer, classify, organize, collect, display, compare, and determine whether fact or opinion. Literal main ideas are stressed and items may require students to apply concepts that are covered in Level 1.

Level 3 requires deep knowledge. Students are encouraged to go beyond the text and are asked to explain, generalize, or connect ideas. Students must be able to support their thinking, citing references from the text or other sources. Items may involve abstract theme identification, inferences between or across passages, students' application of prior knowledge, or text support for analytical judgments to be made.

Level 4 requires complex reasoning, planning, developing, and thinking most likely over an extended period of time, such as comparing multiple works by the same author or from the same time period. The extended time period is not a distinguishing factor if the required work is only repetitive and doesn't require applying a significant conceptual understanding and higher order thinking.

Copyright © 2012 by abcschoolhouse.com

MATH

Level 1 - Recall: this level involves the recall of information (fact, definition, term, or property), the use of a procedure, or applying an algorithm or formula. It also includes one-step word problems, and other specifications unique to content standards.

Level 2 - Skills and Concepts: this level involves demonstrating conceptual understanding through models and explanations, comparing and classifying information, estimating, and interpreting data from a simple graph. A Level 2 response requires students to make some decisions, such as how to approach the problem or activity.

Level 3 - Strategic Thinking: this level involves reasoning, planning, and using evidence to solve a problem or algorithm. Students would be asked at level 3 to make and test conjectures, interpret information from a complex graph, solve complex problems, explain concepts, use concepts to solve non-routine problems, and provide mathematical justifications when more than one response or approach is possible.

Level 4 - Extended Thinking: this level requires complex reasoning, planning, and thinking generally over extended periods of time, but not time spent only on repetitive tasks. At level four, students may be asked to relate concepts to other content areas or to real-world applications in new situations.

Copyright © 2012 by abcschoolhouse.com

WRITING

Level 1 requires the student to write or recite simple facts. This writing or recitation does not include complex synthesis or analysis, but basic ideas.

Level 2 requires some mental processing, such as beginning to connect ideas using a simple organizational structure. At this level, students are engaged in first draft writing for a limited number of purposes and audiences. Students are beginning to connect ideas using a single organizational structure such as composing a short, accurate summary.

Level 3 requires some higher-level mental processing. Students are developing multi-paragraph compositions that may include complex data structures or demonstrate some synthesis and analysis. Revisions were made to their writing to improve precision of language used and to produce a logical progression of ideas.

Level 4 requires higher-level thinking as its central component. Multi-paragraph compositions demonstrate synthesis, analysis, and evaluation of complex ideas or themes and evidence of a deep awareness of purpose and audience. Synthesis and analysis of information from multiple sources often includes identifying the complexities, discrepancies, and/or differences in perspectives found in each medium.

Copyright © 2012 by abcschoolhouse.com

What do activities at the different levels look like?

Knowledge/Remembering Level:

Learning targets begin with phrases such as:

- Students will name ...
- Students will label ...
- Students will list ...
- Students will define ...

Learning activities would look like:

- reciting the ABC's
- tracing letters over dotted lines
- copying definitions of vocabulary words
- spelling practice
- fill in the blank worksheets

Questions could sound like:

- Who is the main character?
- Where is the story setting?
- What did the main character do?

Copyright © 2012 by abcschoolhouse.com

What do activities at the different levels look like?

Comprehension/Understanding Level:

Learning targets begin with phrases such as:

Students will paraphrase …

Students will explain …

Students will illustrate …

Students will give examples of…

Learning activities would look like:

- matching letters to pictures that begin with that letter sound

- using vocabulary/spelling words in a sentence

- summarizing a story

- identifying which formula to use in solving a math problem

Questions could sound like:

What was this story about?

Why did the main character react in the way he did?

What kind of person was the main character?

Copyright © 2012 by abcschoohouse.com

What do activities at the different levels look like?

Application/Applying Level:

Learning targets begin with phrases such as:

Students will demonstrate ...

Using knowledge students will solve ...

Using information students will prepare ...

Students will discuss...

Learning activities would look like:

- illustration of, or dramatization of a scene from the story
- answering multiple choice questions from a graph
- writing a book report
- creating a diorama of a habitat

Questions could sound like:

How are the characters in this story similar to you and your friends?

Share with a neighbor the sequence of the story events?

How would you approach the same situation?

What do activities at the different levels look like?

Analysis/Analyzing Level:

Learning targets begin with phrases such as:

Students will differentiate between ...

Students will analyze and infer...

Students will reduce the materials and outline ...

Students will deconstruct...

Learning activities would look like:

- using Venn Diagrams or T-graphs to compare and contrast
- creating survey questions for a data analysis project
- completing hands-on science experiments
- written essays
- solving probability questions

Questions could sound like:

How are these situations similar and different?

How could you integrate what we learned today into your daily life?

What questions would you ask to determine the outcome?

Copyright © 2012 by abcschoolhouse.com

What do activities at the different levels look like?

Synthesis/Evaluating Level:

Learning targets begin with phrases such as:

Students will design ...

Students will devise a new...

Students will revise this work and integrate ...

Students will critique...

Learning activities could look like:

- using research to write a fact-based persuasive essay
- supporting and defending hypothesis
- students plan and engage in debate
- drawing or dramatizing an advertisement

Questions could sound like:

What moral might the author of the story have been trying to convey & how does this compare to our last story?

What could the character have done differently?

Based on what you know about …. how are these character types usually depicted in literature?

Copyright © 2012 by abcschoolhouse.com

What do activities at the different levels look like?

Evaluation/Creating Level:

Learning targets begin with phrases such as:

Students will evaluate ...

Students will use given criteria to evaluate...

Students will construct ...

Students will design...

Learning activities could look like:

- students will use research to write an article

- students create a map of trade routes and explain the implication of each route

- students will design a form of green energy

- students will generate a plan for a school practice and debate reasons for its implementation

Questions could sound like:

Why did you create ... and what is its importance?

Why did you choose ... as your topic and how did you conduct the research?

Copyright © 2012 by abcschoohouse.com

Knowledge

- recall
- identify
- name
- list
- recognize

Knowledge

. recall

. identify

. name

. list

. recognize

Cheeses of the World:
1. Swiss
2. Brie
3. Gouda
4. Feta
5.
6.

Copyright © 2012 by abcschoolhouse.com

Comprehension

- summarize
- explain
- represent
- illustrate
- categorize

Comprehension

. summarize

. explain

. represent

. illustrate

. categorize

Copyright © 2012 by abcschoohouse.com

Application

- apply
- use
- implement
- demonstrate
- prepare

Application

- apply
- use
- implement
- demonstrate
- prepare

Analysis

- analyze
- infer
- deconstruct
- outline
- differentiate

Analysis

- analyze
- infer
- deconstruct
- outline
- differentiate

Copyright © 2012 by abcschoohouse.com

Synthesis

- design
- invent
- construct
- integrate
- hypothesize

Synthesis

- design
- invent
- construct
- integrate
- hypothesize

Evaluation

- judge
- evaluate
- critique
- compare
- test

Evaluation

- judge
- evaluate
- critique
- compare
- test

Remembering

- recall
- identify
- name
- list
- recognize

Remembering

- recall
- identify
- name
- list
- recognize

Copyright © 2012 by abcschoohouse.com

Understanding

- summarize
- explain
- represent
- illustrate
- categorize

Understanding

- summarize
- explain
- represent
- illustrate
- categorize

Applying

- apply
- use
- implement
- demonstrate
- prepare

Applying

- apply
- use
- implement
- demonstrate
- prepare

Analyzing

- analyze
- infer
- deconstruct
- outline
- differentiate

Analyzing

. analyze

. infer

. deconstruct

. outline

. differentiate

Copyright © 2012 by abcschoohouse.com

Evaluating

- judge
- evaluate
- critique
- compare
- test

Evaluating

. judge

. evaluate

. critique

. compare

. test

Suggestions

Copyright © 2012 by abcschoohouse.com

Creating

- design
- invent
- construct
- integrate
- hypothesize

Creating

. design

. invent

. construct

. integrate

. hypothesize

Copyright © 2012 by abcschoohouse.com

DOK Level 1

- recall
- identify
- name
- list
- recognize

DOK Level 1

. recall

. identify

. name

. list

. recognize

Cheeses of the World:
1. Swiss
2. Brie
3. Gouda
4. Feta
5.
6.

Copyright © 2012 by abcschoohouse.com

DOK Level 2

- summarize
- infer
- estimate
- interpret
- organize

DoK Level 2

- summarize
- infer
- estimate
- interpret
- organize

DOK Level 3

- explain
- generalize
- reason
- plan
- develop

DOK Level 3

- explain
- generalize
- reason
- plan
- develop

DOK Level 4

- create
- integrate
- evaluate
- connect
- invent

DOK Level 4

- create
- integrate
- evaluate
- connect
- invent

Copyright © 2012 by abcschoolhouse.com

Cheeses of the World:
1. Swiss
2. Brie
3. Gouda
4. Feta
5.
6.

At the Pond by Frog

Suggestions

Copyright © 2012 by abcschoolhouse.com

Copyright © 2012 by abcschoolhouse.com

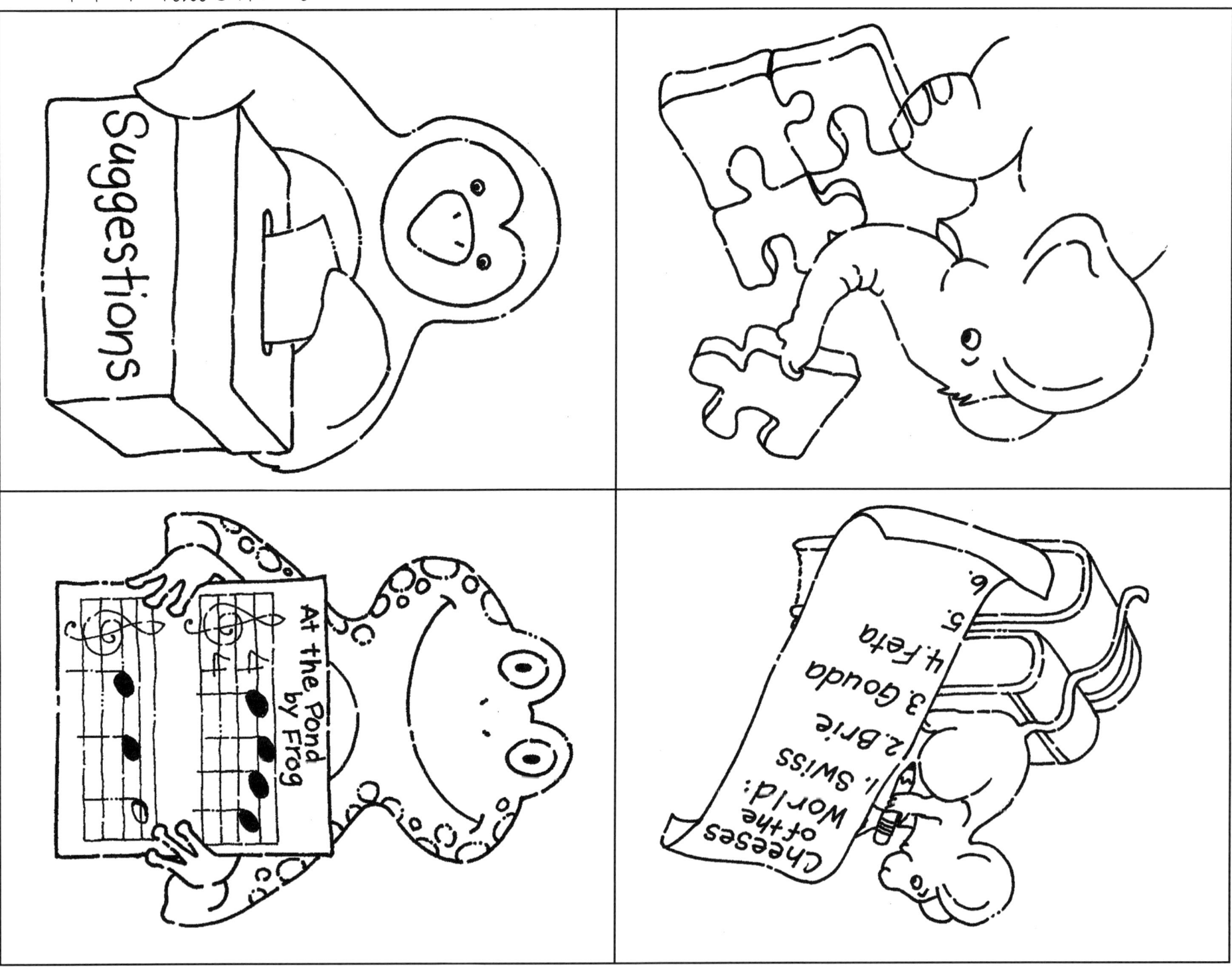

Suggestions

At the Pond by Frog

Cheeses of the World:
1. Swiss
2. Brie
3. Gouda
4. Feta
5.
6.

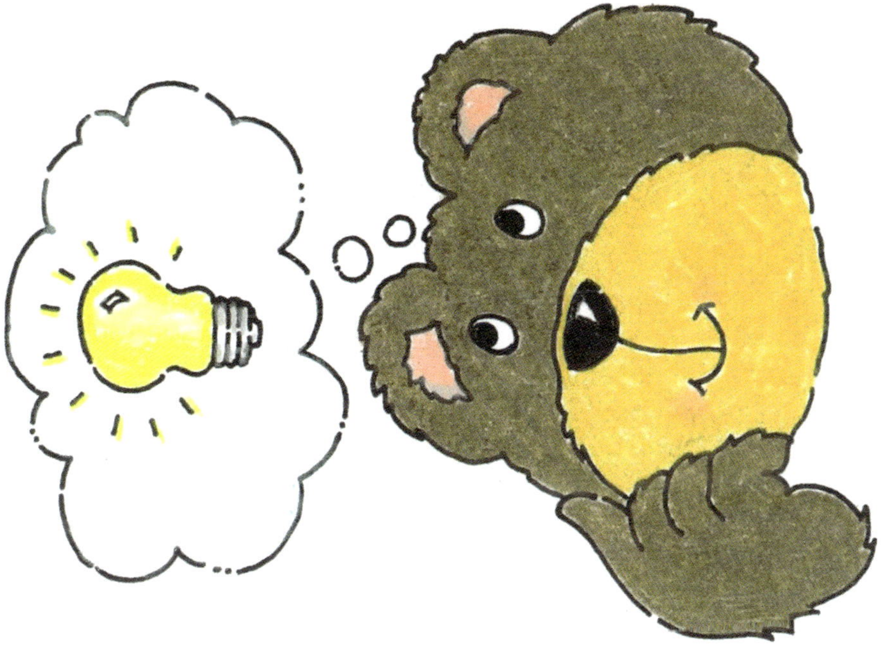

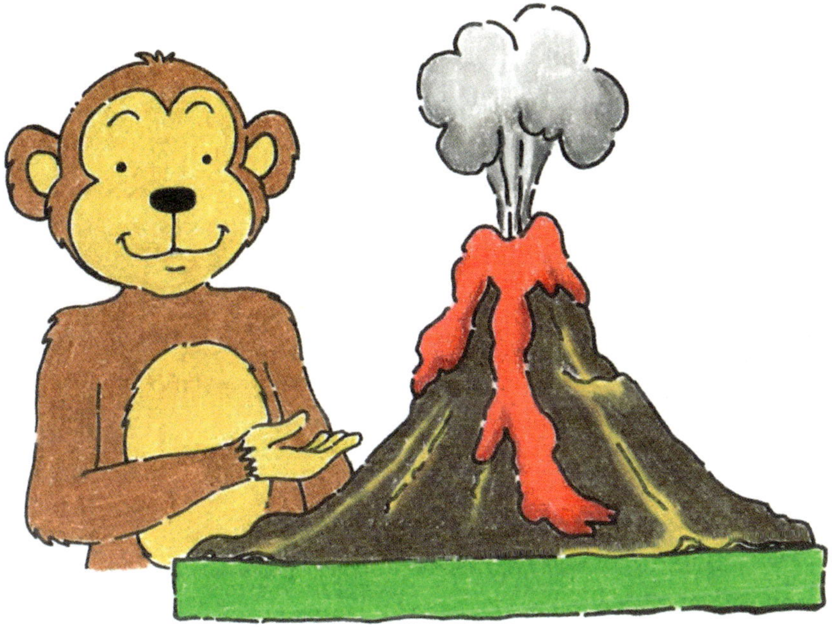

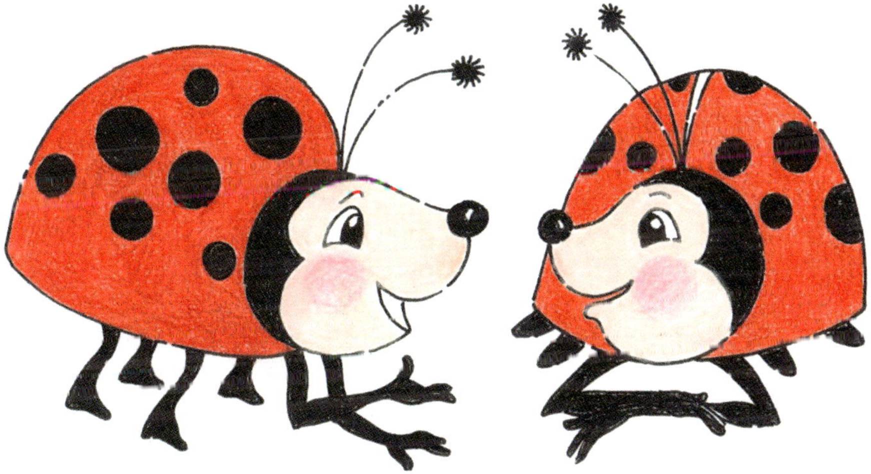

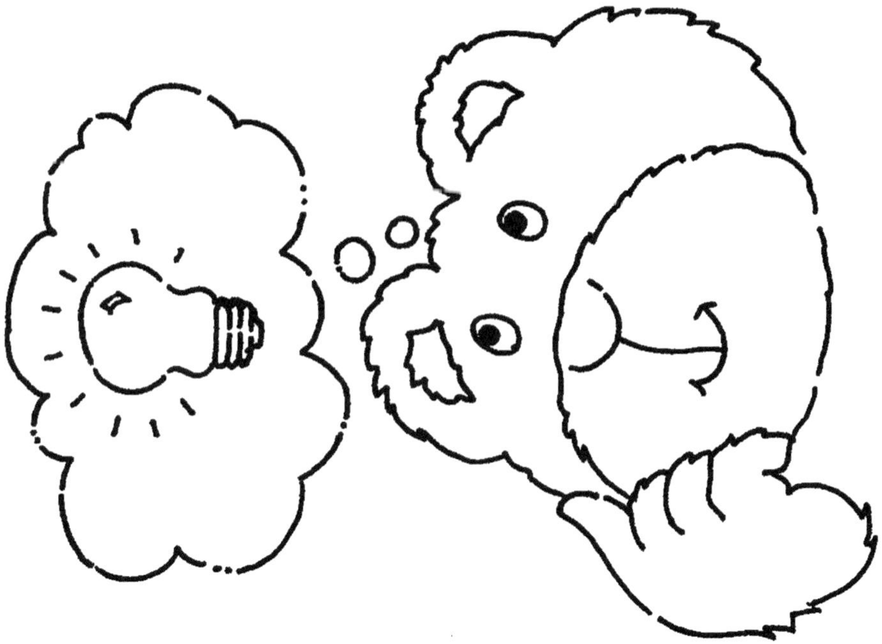

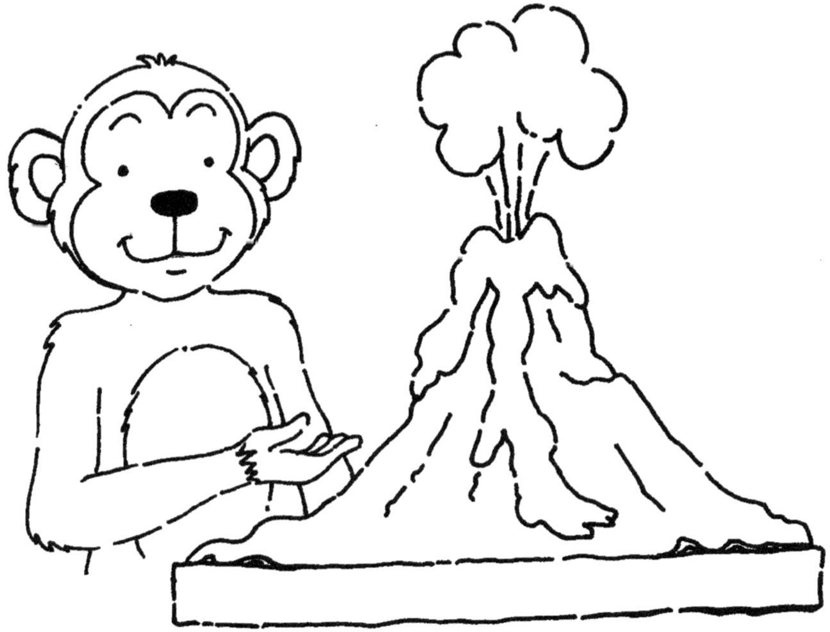

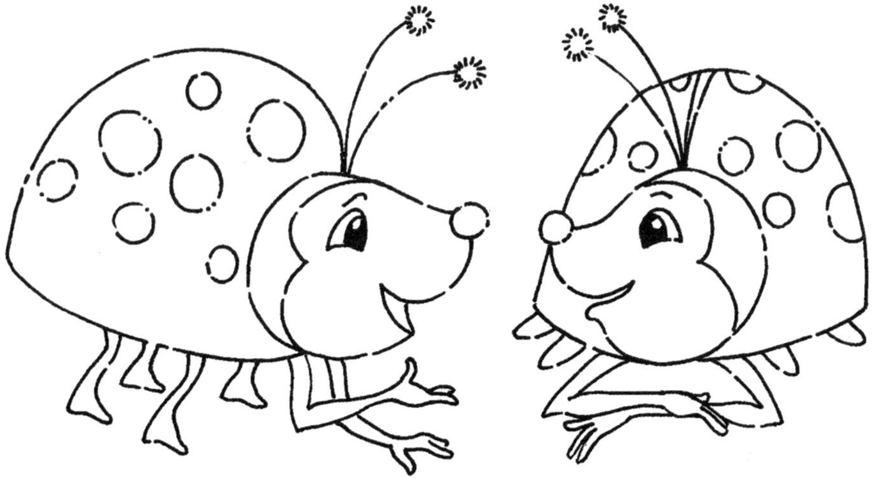

Printed in Great Britain
by Amazon.co.uk, Ltd.,
Marston Gate.